WORLD*focus*
Brazil
DAVID MARSHALL

Contents

Introduction

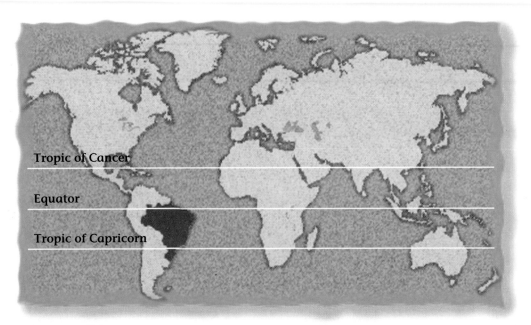

Tropic of Cancer

Equator

Tropic of Capricorn

It is difficult to imagine the size of Brazil. It is the largest country in the continent of South America. It is also the fourth largest country in the world, with an area of 8,512,000 square kilometres. It is 35 times larger than the UK and more than 15 times larger than France.

△ Where is Brazil?

Because of its size Brazil is a land of huge contrasts. There is still uncharted jungle in the Amazon **rain forest**, where over a million different animals and plants live. Some of the plants have great medical value. There are also vast farms in Brazil with orange groves that stretch as far as the eye can see, and crowded cities along the coastline.

▽ Large areas of northeast Brazil suffer from drought, when little, or sometimes no rain falls in a year. Cactus is used to feed the animals.

The Amazon River rises high in the Andes Mountains and flows east to the Atlantic Ocean. On the way, more than a thousand tributaries flow into the river, swelling its size until at times it looks like an inland sea.

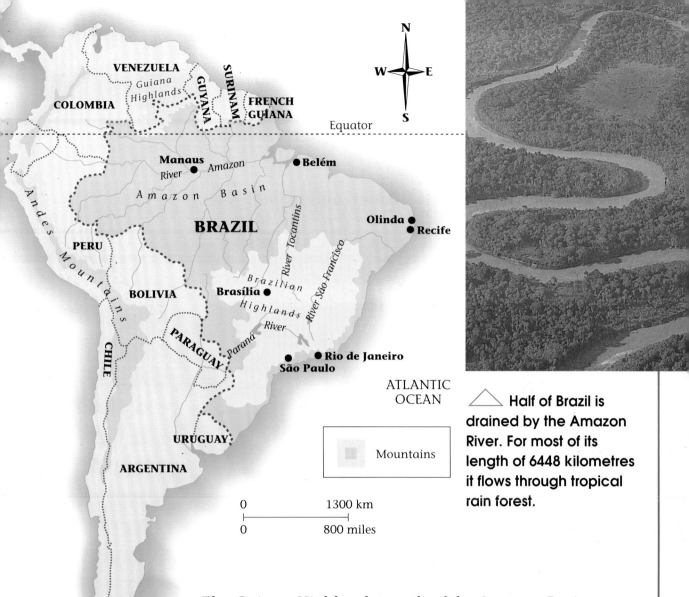

The main features of Brazil's landscape.

Half of Brazil is drained by the Amazon River. For most of its length of 6448 kilometres it flows through tropical rain forest.

The Guiana Highlands, north of the Amazon Basin, have Brazil's highest peaks. Pico de Neblina, or 'Cloudy Peak', is 3014 metres high. The Brazilian Highlands lie to the east and south. This vast plateau is divided by fertile valleys and mountain ranges.

Across the whole of Brazil the climate is varied. In the south the winters are quite cool and sometimes it even snows. In the northeast it is always very hot and the land often looks like a desert. But in the tropical rain forest area of the Amazon Basin, you find one of the steadiest climates in the world. Temperatures here are always about 27°C to 29°C, and it rains all the year round. This type of climate is called **equatorial** because it occurs in areas on the Equator, which passes through the Amazon Basin in the north of Brazil.

The people

Over 150 million people live in Brazil. Throughout Brazil's history, people have come from all over the world to settle there. The population is a mixture of peoples. As well as native **Amerindians**, who have always lived in Brazil, there are European descendants, black Africans brought to Brazil as slaves, and some Japanese. Brazil has the second largest black African population of any country. Many of the different races and peoples have intermarried, which means that Brazilians are one of the most varied peoples in the world.

The first **colonists** from Europe were the Portuguese, who arrived in 1500. At that time there were around 5 million Amerindians in Brazil. Now there are fewer than 200,000.

▷ Salvador is a typical Brazilian city. This photograph shows a favela in the foreground and skyscrapers behind.

Thousands of Amerindians were killed by the settlers. They were made to work as slaves and many died because they were cruelly treated. Others died after catching European diseases. Their bodies had no natural resistance to these diseases. The Amerindians of the forest still live by hunting and gathering food and also by farming. They have kept their old, traditional way of life, but sometimes they use modern farming techniques.

Every year thousands of new settlers still come to Brazil. The fastest growing city is São Paulo. It has the world's largest Japanese community outside Japan.

In Brazil there is a huge difference between the lives of rich and poor people. Over 20 per cent of the Brazilian people cannot read and write. In Britain it is less than 5 per cent. Today over 70 per cent of Brazilians live in the cities. All the major cities have huge shanty towns, known as **favelas** (slums), where poor people put up houses on spare land.

The main religion of Brazil is Roman Catholicism. This was brought to Brazil by the Portuguese. There are still Amerindian religions in parts of Brazil. Some Amerindians believe in spiritualism, which means believing in spirits of people, trees, animals or waterfalls. Some of the black African people brought their own beliefs to Brazil, which they still hold today.

△ Many black Africans in Brazil are descended from slaves who were brought to Brazil over 300 years ago.

Where do people live?

Over 90 per cent of Brazilians live in one-third of the country – mainly in the south and along the coast. The major cities are São Paulo and Rio de Janeiro. São Paulo has a population of over 14,000,000 and is the second largest city in the world. Rio de Janeiro is featured in many travel films because of its beautiful position. It lies just where the hills of the tropical forests roll down to the long sandy beaches of the Atlantic coast.

△ **The cathedral in Brasília is just one of the exciting buildings in Brazil's new capital.**

The government of Brazil wanted to encourage people to live in the vast interior of the country. In 1956 it decided to develop a brand new capital city there, called Brasília. The government hoped that moving the capital from Rio de Janeiro on the coast to the centre of Brazil would help to develop the rest of Brazil. Brasília was built at breakneck speed in three years and it opened on 21 April 1960. It now has a population of over 1,500,000.

Most of the people who live in the countryside live on patches of land too small to produce enough to feed their families. Just a few large landowners own enormous expanses of land. Many people are employed on these large farms, but they are usually paid very little. Since the 1950s thousands of people have moved from villages into the cities of Brazil looking for work. They believe that life in towns will be better.

Brazil's cities are very overcrowded and there are shortages of houses and jobs. In an attempt to solve these problems the government has moved some families away from the cities. People have been moved into the Amazon Basin in **colonization** projects. They have been given small farms on land which was once rain forest. Trees have been felled and the land cleared for raising crops. However, the soil is poor and there are few **nutrients** to feed the growing crops. After two or three years, the soil is exhausted and may be washed away by heavy rainfall. Many of the people have moved back again to the cities after a few years.

There is a lot of land available for farming in Brazil. It should not be difficult for the government to help families who want to farm. It could be done by giving out some land and lending people money to buy seeds and tools. The government has often promised to help in this way, but never has. It prefers to lend money to large landowners. Big landowners do not want changes. They are afraid that if the poor have their own land it will become difficult for them to find cheap labour. As a result the rich farmers get richer and the poor landless farmers become poorer.

△ **People who move to the cities have to take any job they can find.**

Agriculture

You can grow almost any crop in Brazil because the climate is so varied. Although many people think of coffee when they think of Brazil, other crops (like soya beans and sugar cane) are just as important. Cacão, tobacco, maize, rice, cotton and some rubber are also grown. Brazil is the biggest **exporter** of oranges in the world. Sugar cane is used to make an alcohol mixture which is used as fuel for cars!

In the 19th century rubber was the most important crop in Brazil. It was collected from trees in the forests. In 1876 some seedlings were smuggled out of Brazil to London. They were used to start rubber growing in other countries, mainly in the **Far East**, where the rubber was grown on **plantations**. Brazil's rubber industry could not compete with the new plantations.

Brazil has a huge farming industry. It grows food and raises animals to feed the people of Brazil and for export. Crops are also grown as **raw materials** for Brazil's industries. About one-third of Brazil's exports come from farming.

Many of the people who live in the countryside do not benefit from this huge farming business. They are the landless labourers who work on the farms and plantations. Over 12 million people who live in Brazil's countryside are landless, or have so little land that they cannot grow enough food to survive. Over half of all the land in Brazil is owned by only one-tenth of the population. It is this small number of Brazilians who mainly benefit from Brazil's rich agriculture.

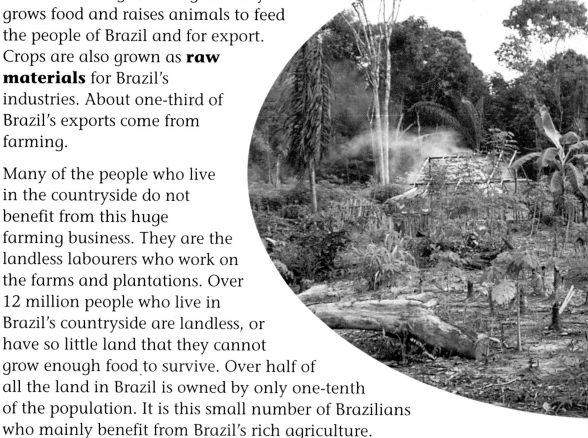

▽ This area was once covered by trees. A farmer is now trying to make a living off the land.

These Zebu cattle have been brought from India. They thrive in Brazil's climate.

There is plenty of food in Brazil, but people still go hungry. In the towns and cities they may not earn enough money to be able to buy food. The wealth is not evenly distributed in Brazil. In the countryside farmers may not be able to grow enough food to feed themselves and their families. Some of Brazil's produce is also exported. This earns money that is used to repay Brazil's enormous debts to foreign countries.

Over half of Brazil is covered by forest. The Amazon rain forest has the world's greatest number of tropical **hardwoods**. These trees are very valuable. The search for **mahogany** by illegal logging gangs is threatening vast areas of the Amazon forest. The Brazilian government has encouraged landless families and people from the cities to move to land cleared from the forests. This land is often not suitable for growing crops. Also, these people are sometimes driven off their land by wealthy ranchers who then raise cattle on the land.

Industry

The Itaipu dam contains enough concrete to build a 350-storey skyscraper every day for five years.

Since the 1950s the Brazilian government has led a massive industrial development programme. Brazil's main export used to be coffee, but now industry produces two-thirds of all exports. Brazil's main exports are cars, machinery, ships, aircraft, shoes and iron ore.

Belo Horizonte, São Paulo and Rio de Janeiro form a triangle, where most of Brazil's manufacturing takes place (see map on page 11).

Brazil has enormous natural wealth. Iron ore, phosphates, uranium, copper, manganese, bauxite and coal are all waiting to be mined. The government does not have the money to pay for these projects. Brazil is also now into its second gold boom, with gold being found both underground and in rivers in the Amazon region.

Nearly all the energy in Brazil is produced by **hydroelectric** power stations. To harness energy, a huge dam is built across a river. The dams at Tucuruî in the Amazon Basin and Itaipu on the Paranà River are two of the largest in the world. The giant Itaipu dam cost $20 billion to build. The walls of the dam are the height of a 60-storey skyscraper. When a dam is built a large area of land is flooded. At Itaipu dam, many people were forced off their land as the water rose.

There are many new mines and refineries in Brazil. The picture shows the iron ore mine at Carajàs, which is one of the biggest.

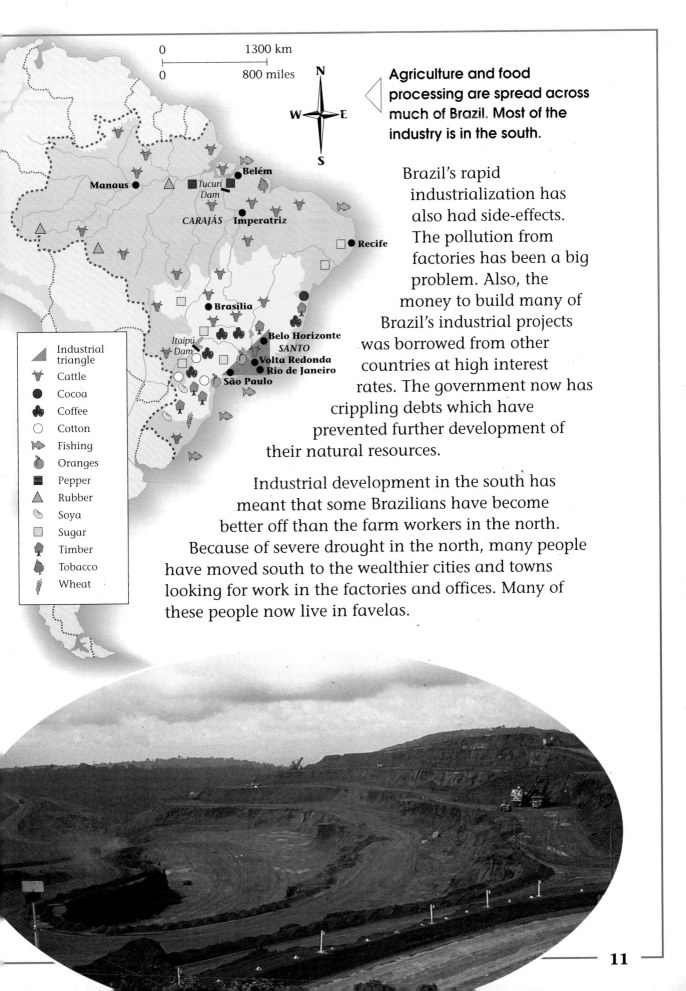

Map scale:
0 — 1300 km
0 — 800 miles

Map legend:
- Industrial triangle
- Cattle
- Cocoa
- Coffee
- Cotton
- Fishing
- Oranges
- Pepper
- Rubber
- Soya
- Sugar
- Timber
- Tobacco
- Wheat

Map labels: Manaus, Belém, Tucuí Dam, CARAJÁS, Imperatriz, Recife, Brasília, Itaipú Dam, Belo Horizonte, SANTO, Volta Redonda, Rio de Janeiro, São Paulo

Agriculture and food processing are spread across much of Brazil. Most of the industry is in the south.

Brazil's rapid industrialization has also had side-effects. The pollution from factories has been a big problem. Also, the money to build many of Brazil's industrial projects was borrowed from other countries at high interest rates. The government now has crippling debts which have prevented further development of their natural resources.

Industrial development in the south has meant that some Brazilians have become better off than the farm workers in the north. Because of severe drought in the north, many people have moved south to the wealthier cities and towns looking for work in the factories and offices. Many of these people now live in favelas.

The rich and the poor

In Brazil there are two worlds: a rich world and a poor world.

In the rich world people are very well off. They work in industry and business, or as doctors, lawyers or accountants, or are big landowners or merchants. They are better off than most people in the developed world.

In the poor world people are very poor. They do not have enough to eat, they do not have enough money to buy clothes or shoes, or to pay for medicines or schooling. They get ill easily and they die younger. The poorest people live in the countryside and in the favelas of the towns and cities.

The government has tried to use Brazil's natural riches to make money to pay off its huge debts and to make life better for all Brazilians. It has encouraged industry and developed agriculture. This has been quite successful, but the people who have benefited have mainly been those who were already wealthy. Poor people are not much better off, even though Brazil as a whole has become richer.

Most favelas have no rubbish collections. Here in Recife, a pig feeds amongst the rubbish at the side of the main road.

There have been some huge industrial developments in the countryside. One is at Carajás in the north of Brazil, in Amazonia. Here there is an iron ore mine, logging from the rain forest, an aluminium **smelter** and a good railway system. The Carajás development involved cutting down an area of forest as big as France, in less than ten years. Hundreds of thousands of the poorest Brazilians came to Carajás from all over the country in search of work and land. A nearby village called Imperatríz became a town of nearly half a million people. There were no plans to cope with this sudden growth, and the city grew with no health or sanitation system. While it was being built, Carajás offered some jobs. But there were not enough long-term jobs for all the people who flocked to Imperatríz.

Deforestation means that many Amerindians lose their homes.

The destruction of the rain forest, known as **deforestation**, is seen as a disaster by most people in the rest of the world. For the Amerindians who have lived in the forest for generations, it can mean the end of their traditional way of life. The government has a policy known as **demarcation** which tries to protect Indian reservations from development. However, many Indian groups have not been able to register their lands, and developers seem to be able to ignore this protection.

Brazil needs to find a way to preserve its environment at the same time as making the best use of its natural resources for the benefit of all its people.

Recife

Recife is Brazil's fourth largest city, with a population of over 1,200,000. It is the capital of the state of Pernambuco in the northeast of Brazil. Recife is a port and is sometimes called the Venice of Brazil, because it is a city of water and bridges. Nearby is Recife's sister town of Olinda, which was Brazil's capital before Rio de Janeiro and Brasília.

Recife is big and modern, but more difficult to travel around than many other large cities. The centre is a mixture of high-rise offices, old colonial churches and crowded markets. It is easy for strangers to get lost in the maze of winding, one-way streets. Some of Brazil's most famous artists live in Recife, and it is well known for its painting, sculpture, dance, music and festivals.

△ A child sits by the road in a favela, in the Entre Apulso area of Recife.

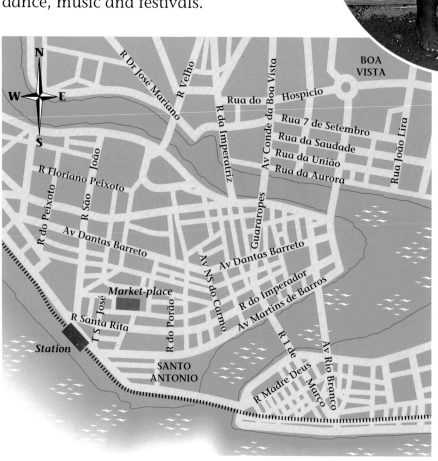

◁ Recife.

Recife has an airport where many flights from Europe land. Flights bringing Europeans have led to a great many developments for tourists and rich landowners. New nightclubs, restaurants and hotels have grown up round the beaches of Boa Viagem. The beaches are Recife's biggest tourist attraction.

In the last few years, severe drought in the northeast has caused many crops to fail. Nearly half the sugar-cane harvest has been lost. Many people have had to travel long distances searching for water. The drought has led to over a million people, especially men, moving away from the countryside into the cities, looking for work. Even cities like Recife are suffering from constant water shortages and rationing. New favelas for the migrants have grown in no time at all and appear almost everywhere. Favela houses are really just shacks, usually made from wood and corrugated metal sheets, plastic and cardboard. Very few favelas have running water, electricity or sewage systems.

△ Favelas have been built on spare land in Recife. You can see the tall buildings of the city centre in the distance.

City life

In Recife, as in all the major cities of Brazil, there is a big difference between the lives of the rich and poor people.

Recife is a port and many people work in offices that are connected with imports and exports. The airport employs hundreds of people in many different jobs. Recife's banks open for just a few hours every day. When they are open they are very busy. All through the day you can see business people hurrying to and fro. Most of the shops open at 8 a.m. and do not close until 7 p.m. The bigger shopping centres stay open until 10 p.m. so that people with money can buy what they need in the evenings when it is cooler.

 A Brazilian paints his jangada, or fishing boat, in Recife.

Most jobs for people in the poor districts of Recife are casual. There is never enough work to go round. People have to find any work they can. It is hard to earn enough money to live on. The poorer districts are often the farthest away from work. People who do have jobs have to leave their houses as early as 5 a.m. or 6 a.m. to take two or three buses to the city centre.

Brazil has a small fishing industry and most of it is in the north near Recife. Every morning Edison Nantes arrives at his local market with the fish he has caught that morning. Edison owns a traditional Brazilian fishing boat called a jangada. Jangadas used to be made from logs lashed together. Edison's is made from plastic tubes which do not need painting.

△ **This boy is selling slices of melon from his stall in Recife's market-place.**

There are stalls and markets all over Recife. There are many craftspeople who make pots, tableware, jewellery and ornaments. The local market stalls have things to buy, for people with money. They are always well stocked with fresh produce despite the drought.

Claudia, Edison's wife, is typical of many of the poorer women in Recife. They work as maids, cleaners or cooks in the houses of the better off. Claudia spends her day washing, cleaning and cooking for a family who work in one of the offices in the city. The richer people of Recife do not buy washing machines or dishwashers. It is cheaper to employ servants like Claudia. The very rich often have several servants – housemaids, a chauffeur, and sometimes a gardener. Those who live in big houses often employ armed guards to patrol their area.

School

In the poorer parts of Recife many people work part-time or have no job at all. Children have to try to earn some money, often by begging. Many do not go to school.

Many children in Recife shine shoes, clean windscreens or sell food in the streets. In the countryside outside Recife, they work on farms or in the home.

Over half of the children in Brazil go to private schools. Their parents are the people who have jobs in offices, banks or factories in the cities, or who are landowners and farmers. There are many private schools in Recife. There are also 'self-help' schools. These have been started by poor people to make sure that their children have some education. These schools do not have many facilities like books. In school, as in the rest of life in Brazil, there is a rich world and a poor world.

 A primary school class in Recife's neighbouring town, Olinda.

Many adults who went to poor schools, or left school at a very early age, cannot read or write, or have only very basic skills. The government knows this is a major problem. In order to help it has set up adult education classes in the evenings. However, most people cannot see the point of going to them because they will not always lead to a job. There are simply not enough jobs for everyone.

In parts of Brazil, Amerindian groups have their own education or training systems. The Kayapo and Shavante Indians live in reservations often far from their original lands. Their population is only about 3000 in total. The men of the village have a council meeting and debating session every evening. During this meeting village decisions are made. The boys are allowed to sit in and learn from their elders. By teaching their children themselves, they can keep their traditions alive. The younger generations will know how to follow the tribal way of life. If they go to government schools they may be influenced by Western ideas and modern lifestyles.

△ **Children at this school in northeast Brazil have to wear a uniform.**

Spare time

In Recife most people have spare time at the weekend, which they spend on the beach. On Sundays in particular everyone seems to be on the beach or sea front. There are parties with dancing and singing. Adults and children dance in the street in the midday sun. Some of the dances are called the samba, the lambada and the bossa nova. In the northeast a special form of the samba, called frevo, has grown up over the years. The frevo is danced by solo dancers holding a small umbrella or parasol in one hand. It is a very fast and exhausting dance which has many knee bends and kicks rather like a Russian Cossack dance.

The most important spare time activity for the people of Brazil is preparing for the carnival. In Recife, groups called Blocos practise all year round to be ready for the next carnival. The Blocos have names like 'We Suffer but We Can Dance!' One Bloco has thousands of members, and they all get involved in the celebrations.

▽ The streets are crowded for days during carnival time in Recife.

Originally the carnival was on Shrove Tuesday, the day before Lent. The idea was to use up all the energy, food, drink and fun that would have to be forgotten during the sombre period of Lent. Today it is a much longer event, lasting at least four days. It is also much noisier. The streets are packed with people in costumes, drinking, dancing and singing. An essential part of any carnival celebration is drinking. The drinks are ice-cold beer and 'cachaça', a strong drink made from sugar-cane.

△ The splendour of the Rio Carnival, the biggest carnival in Brazil.

These carnivals in Recife are open to everyone, there is no entry fee.

Without doubt, football and volleyball are the most important parts of many young people's lives. Recife has three football teams. Brazil has won the World Cup three times. Also, the country has perhaps the world's best player ever: Pelé. If Brazilians are not playing football, many will be watching. The Maracana stadium in Rio is the largest in the world. It is probably the noisiest and most colourful, too.

Katia's day

Katia is eleven years old. She moved to Recife four years ago with her family when the drought ruined the farm they worked on. Now she lives in a favela with her mother, Maria, and her four younger brothers and sisters. They are Paulo (nine), Claudia (seven), Patricia (four) and the baby, Pedro (one). Their father, also called Pedro, now lives with his brother in São Paulo. They are working in a new factory there. Sometimes Katia's father can send them some money, but it is never enough to live on.

△ Unlike Katia's mother who has a cart, these men sell their fruit and vegetables from a stall.

Katia is always up by 6 a.m. Everybody gets up early in Brazil. Her first job is to make coffee for everyone. Next the younger children have to be looked after.

Because she is the oldest child, Katia helps her mother to prepare the sweetcorn that they will take into the city to sell on the street. Katia's aunt collects Patricia and Pedro and takes them to her house. Katia takes the other children to school by 8.30 a.m. and then helps to wheel the cart to their usual pitch on a street corner. She looks after the cart while her mother goes to collect laundry. The family washes other people's laundry to earn some more money.

At noon, Katia collects the children from school – their education is over for the day. She gives them their lunch of rice and beans before taking them to her aunt's house on the other side of the town. She then walks back to her mother's cart to take her some lunch, before walking 4 kilometres to school. She cannot afford to go by bus. The long walk means that she is often late for school, which begins at 1 p.m.

△ **These children are playing beside a favela in Recife.**

Katia's school 'day' only lasts for three hours. She studies Portuguese, history, geography and maths. Like a lot of her friends, Katia enjoys school. But she only makes poor progress because she cannot study at home and her family cannot afford to buy pens, paper or books.

Just after 5 p.m. Katia arrives home after collecting the children from their aunt's. Katia keeps an eye on them as they play, while she starts another job, washing the laundry her mother has collected earlier in the day. At around 8 p.m., after they have eaten, she takes all the children with her to meet their mother and helps to bring the cart home. Her mother carries on with the laundry so that Katia can wash and bathe the children by pouring cold water over them from tin cans. Finally, Katia goes to bed, at about 9 p.m.

Travelling around

Traffic crossing the Boa Vista bridge in Recife.

In the city centre of Recife, there is constant bustle. The traffic is always busy and there are crowds of people. The pavements are packed with people setting up their stalls and carts. They sell everything, from kitchen equipment to music. Stall holders call out to passers-by.

There is always a lot of music. Shops and stalls blare out all the time. The 'sound waggons' add to the street noise. These are massive loudspeakers on wheels, some as big as lorries. They are used to advertise goods, church services, or local politicians.

The streets are full of people selling. Children carry trays or handfuls of goods. They run after passers-by, clamouring for a sale. There are piles of fruit from the nearby countryside. Stall holders spray water on the fruit to keep it looking attractive, and to drive off the flies!

To get into, or away from the city centre, people crowd onto Recife's very good bus service. You can get to almost anywhere in Brazil by bus from Recife, as well as just around the city. Everyone has to go through a turnstile at the back of the bus when they pay to get on. Small children often crawl under the turnstile and travel free! There are taxis on all the major streets which will take you through the maze of winding streets in the city centre.

The buildings in the centre of Recife are a mixture of the old, grand Portuguese style, and new blocks built in the 1970s. Many of the old-style buildings are crumbling. At night many people sleep near the cathedral or in doorways. In the daytime these people beg, or if they are lucky, do odd jobs. Farther out, in the newer suburbs, people usually live in blocks of flats. Because the climate is so warm, children can play outside all year round.

In Recife, favelas are squeezed in almost anywhere, often between other buildings. The paths between the houses are narrow and twisty. There is no need for wide roads because no one owns a car here. In some places there are planks to walk on because the ground is always wet.

▽ Some streets in Recife still have old, Portuguese-style buildings.

Journeys

Brazil has a modern road transport system. Since the 1960's the government has borrowed a lot of money to build new roads, many through the Amazon Basin. The first connected Brasília with Belém in the north. Another carries wood from the logging industry in the forest to the southeast. The latest is the Trans-Amazonian Highway. When it is finished it will go from Recife in the east to the Peruvian border in the west. This highway will be 5000 kilometres long.

In the south of Brazil there is a good local road network. However, in the north and in the Amazon Basin you can only travel locally by walking, or by plane or boat. Many of the roads are not properly made, so when the torrential rains come they are washed away.

Buses are the least expensive way of travelling long distances. The regional bus services are excellent and they go from city to city. The distances to be covered are huge. If you want to travel by bus from Recife to Belém around the coast in the northern states it will cost about £17, and it will take two days.

The length of time taken to make the journey by road can be shortened to a few hours by going by plane. That is why there are hundreds of small airports all over Brazil. There are even airports in the depths of the Amazon Basin. All the major cities have big international airports. Travel by plane is the most expensive way to travel.

△ These Kaxinawa Indians are making their journey by boat.

▷ Lorries and cars often have to rely on rafts like this to cross Brazil's rivers.

In the Amazon Basin, river transport is still important. For many riverside communities the only link with the nearest town is by river. Because the Amazon River is so large, there are ocean-going ships travelling right up to Manaus in the centre of the forest. There are specially built two-decker boats for long trips. These have enough room for people to hang their hammocks. Many people use canoes for short trips to pick up their provisions.

Not many Brazilians own cars, but those that do have a choice of different types of fuel. Some use petrol and some diesel, but many run their cars on the alcohol fuel produced from sugar-cane.

Looking at Brazil

Brazil today is a wonderful and complex mixture of the old and the new. There are modern cities, with skyscrapers and airports. In the Amazon forest Amerindian tribes follow traditions and a way of life that has not changed for thousands of years. There are rich landowners and huge multinational businesses. There are thousands of poor people living in slums too. Throughout the country's history people have come to Brazil from all over the world, and this has made a rich, colourful mixture of customs and beliefs.

We always have images of a country in our minds, even if we have never actually been there. This book has tried to show many sides of Brazil. It has included some positive ideas and pictures about the country. It has shown what Brazilian people are doing to make a better life for themselves and their families.

▷ The carnival in Olinda.

▽ Brazilian footballers in action.

△ Sunrise over Rio.

▷ Amerindian child swinging in a hammock.

Brazil is a country rich in natural resources. It has enormous reserves of many important minerals, huge forests, and vast rivers. In the last fifty years, as part of an attempt to modernize the country, the government has decided to build a new capital city in Brasília and invest in new industries and roads to exploit this natural wealth. Unfortunately, this has led to Brazil having huge debts to pay to other countries and the cutting down of much of the rain forest. It has also meant that the wealthy landowners have grown richer, and there has been little benefit to the poor people. Oxfam and other development agencies have offered assistance and helped people to organize themselves. Hardworking and determined Brazilians are trying to better their own conditions. By reading this book you will have gained an insight into the lives of Brazilian people today.

Glossary

Amerindians a combination of two words, American and Indian, to describe the original inhabitants of Brazil.

colonists groups of settlers or planters who left their own homes to live in new lands under the rule of their old countries.

colonization when new settlers take over a country, or part of it, and claim it as their own, or for their own country.

deforestation the clearance of all the trees and undergrowth in a forest to make land useable for farming.

demarcation the act of putting down a boundary or a line marking out different areas of land.

equatorial land that is near the equator – the imaginary line that runs round the centre of the earth – and the climate in that region.

exporter a company, or individual, who buys or makes goods to sell abroad and not in their home country.

Far East an area of the world made up of China, Japan, and other countries of East Asia.

favelas the Portugese word for slums, these shanty towns now exist all over Brazil.

hardwoods the wood from a deciduous tree (a tree which sheds its leaves every year – such as an oak) as opposed to wood from conifers.

hydroelectric electricity generated by using water power from dams.

mahogony a dark, very hard wood, used for making furniture.

nutrients anything that contains the food or minerals necessary for life to continue.

plantations an area of land in old colonies, often called an estate, that was cultivated, usually with one crop like cotton or sugar cane.

rain forest the dense tropical forest that grows in the hot, tropical regions of the world where there is always heavy rainfall.

raw materials the basic materials, like wood and iron ore, from which finished goods are made.

Index

About Oxfam in Brazil

Oxfam works with poor people and their organizations in over 80 countries. Oxfam believes that all people have basic rights: to earn a living, and to have food, shelter, health care and education. Oxfam provides relief in emergencies, and gives long-term support to people struggling to build a better life for themselves and their families.

Oxfam's programme in Brazil concentrates on the north-east and the Amazon basin - the country's poorest regions. Oxfam supports landless people, both rural and urban, providing training, legal advice, and agricultural technology. Oxfam also helps people to claim their basic rights, through work with community and women's groups, and with trade unions, strengthening these organizations through leadership training. Oxfam is also helping poor people in Brazil to improve their living conditions by working with local groups - training health educators and literacy workers.

The author and publishers would like to thank the following for their help in preparing this book: The staff in the Recife office of Oxfam; Emma Naylor of the Brazil Desk in Oxfam and the staff of the Latin America and Caribbean Desk; the staff of the Oxfam photo library; and the Oxfam Education staff who commented on early drafts.

The Oxfam Education Catalogue lists a range of other resources on economically developing countries, including Brazil, and issues of development. These materials are produced by Oxfam, by other agencies, and by Development Education Centres. For a copy of the catalogue contact Oxfam, 274 Banbury Road, Oxford OX2 7DZ, phone (0865) 311311, or your national Oxfam office.

Photographic acknowledgements
The author and publishers wish to acknowledge, with thanks, the following photographic sources:

Oxfam/Andrew Couldridge pp2, 4, 9, 15, 27;/Jenny Matthews pp3, 5, 6, 7, 12, 14, 18, 22, 23, 26;/ F. Rubin p8/9, 29;/Tony Gloss pp11, 13; Reportage/Julio Etchart p10; South American Pictures/Tony Morrison pp16, 17, 20, 21, 24, 28; Hutchison Library p19; Andes Press Agency/Carlos Reyes p25; Allsport p28.

The publishers have made every effort to trace the copyright holders, but if they have inadvertently overlooked any, they will be pleased to make the necessary arrangement at the first opportunity.

Cover photograph of an Amerindian child
© Oxfam/Mike Goldwater

Note to the reader - In this book there are some words in the text which are printed in **bold** type. This shows that the word is listed in the glossary on page 30. The glossary gives a brief explanation of words which may be new to you.

First published in Great Britain by Heinemann Library an imprint of Heinemann Publishers (Oxford) Ltd Halley Court, Jordan Hill, Oxford OX2 8EJ

OXFORD LONDON EDINBURGH MADRID ATHENS BOLOGNA PARIS MELBOURNE SYDNEY AUCKLAND SINGAPURE TOKYO IBADAN NAIROBI HARARE GABORONE PORTSMOUTH NH (USA)

© 1994 Heinemann Library

98 97 96 95 94
10 9 8 7 6 5 4 3 2 1

British Library Cataloguing in Publication Data is available from the British Library on request.

ISBN 0 431 07253 1 (Hardback)

ISBN 0 431 07256 6 (Paperback)

Designed and produced by Visual Image
Cover design by Threefold Design

Printed in China